FIRST CENTURY WORDS REVEALED TO TWENTY-FIRST CENTURY BELIEVERS

Analyzing the Dietary Laws

A  Book ©

Robin Gould, D.R.E., LMFT

Copyright © Robin Gould, 2017

Printed in the United States of America

Without limiting the rights under copyright reserved above, no part of this publication may be reproduced, stored in, or introduced into a retrieval system, or transmitted, in any form, or by any means (electronic, mechanical, photocopying, recording, or otherwise), without the prior written permission of the copyright owner.

This booklet is a BEKY Book publication:
Books Encouraging the Kingdom of Yeshua.
www.bekybooks.com

Cover design by Rubel Photography, Mt. Juliet, TN.

Illustrations by Tasha Carthy.

DEDICATION

This book is dedicated to my son, Dominic.

As the first miracle I ever knew, to the joy I experience every day with you in my life, you have made me understand what truly matters.

I love you.

CONTENTS

	Glossary	7
	Introduction	9
1	Nothing Refused	13
2	Seducing Spirits, Lies, and Hypocrisy	23
3	Received with Thanksgiving	29
4	Fulfilled by the Resurrection	33
5	Sanctified Food	37
6	What Goes In, or What Comes Out?	43
7	Conclusion	63
	Questions for Review	65
	Appendix	67
	References	69
	About the Author	71
	Acknowledgements	73

GLOSSARY

Syncretic - a union or attempted fusion of different religions, cultures, or philosophies.

Law of first mention - The hermeneutical rule that first usage of a word solidifies it's meaning throughout the rest of the text.

Hermeneutics - methods of biblical interpretation applying accepted rules of interpretation.

Etymology - the origin and use of a word with discovery of its alteration when transferred to other languages and cultures.

Torah - the first five books of the Bible, misunderstood as "law" in English translations. The Torah is more accurately God's teaching and instruction. It contains topics such as science, history, priestly procedures, civil statutes, ordinances, health, agriculture, commandments, prophecies, prayer, animal husbandry, architecture, civics, and many others. The root word of Torah comes from the Hebrew word *yarah*, which means "to hit the mark." Torah may also be used to refer to all of the Hebrew Bible, or even to its smallest meaning, a procedure. Torah may be used by Messianic Jews to refer to the entire Bible from Genesis to Revelation, for the Torah is the foundation for all the Scriptures. The Prophets point Israel back to the Torah. The Psalms teach one to love the Torah as King David loved it. The Writings teach the consequences of departing from the Torah and the rewards for returning to it. The New Testament brings the Torah to its fullest meaning in the person Yeshua the Messiah, and much of the New Testament quotes the Tanakh.

Sanctified - to be set apart for holy use; to be separate due to holy parameters or behaviors that are compliant with holy standards and expectations.

Mishnah - the codified Jewish Oral Law compiled and finally written down by Judah HaNasi around 200 A.D.; it is composed of six orders (sedarim) and sixty-three tractates.

Talmud - the largest body of Jewish Law and commentary containing the Mishnah, Gemara, and Tosefta. It was not completed until the Medieval Period of history.

Kosher - meats fit to be considered food as written in the dietary food laws of scripture.

Sanhedrin - an authoritative religious assembly or court in the Land of Israel. Although its powers were increased or limited at various times in Jewish history since the return from Babylon, some responsibilities were: supervising the Temple service, deciding as to the harvest tithes, sitting in civil judgment, arranging the calendar, providing correct copies of the Torah roll for the king, and probably for the Temple, deciding all doubtful questions relating to the religious law and rendering the final decision.

Yeshua - Hebrew name for Jesus that means salvation.

INTRODUCTION

Sometimes reading the Bible can feel like watching a tennis match. Heads swing from one side to the other as it can appear that two different competing players wrote it. Often the "God of Law" in the Old Testament and the "God of Love" in the New Testament seem contradictory. Have you ever experienced the Bible like that? If so, this can be a frustrating and scary experience for a committed Believer. When the God we are to trust, attach to, and stake our eternity on is a moving target, this does not cultivate a healthy or secure spiritual condition. If you've ever silently suffered this insecurity, it is time to be delivered from Bible Ping Pong Syndrome.

Believers in Yeshua (Jesus) are thrilled with the simplicity of the "good news" (and rightfully so), but incredibly there is more truth for the committed student to find. For an inquisitive truth seeker, the good news keeps coming. It's even more exciting to realize that the information presented in this book is not new at all. This book retraces a path from the very beginning of the Ancient of Days, good news to celebrate! This celebration obliterates the obstacles fueling the Ping Pong Syndrome. This book can ignite a lamp by which Messiah ceases to be a moving target! The goal is to see the simplicity of the secure attachment He offers those who truly seek Him and to discard all the detours.

The letters from Paul to Timothy and Mark, as well as some of the Gospel accounts, are the focus. These are used as proof texts to support a theological position that following the death, burial, and resurrection of the Messiah, the 1st Century brought with it an end to the Torah dietary laws found in Leviticus 11 and Deuteronomy 14. This theory is that the entire sacrificial system, the Sabbath, and the other laws in the first five books of the Bible were fulfilled and are no longer of use in practical application.

The Bible disputes these assertions about Paul's teachings as they relate to the Temple. Paul, after his vision of the resurrected Messiah, went to the Temple bringing offerings and sacrifices.

> So Paul went to the Temple the next day with the other men. They had already started the purification ritual, so he publicly announced the date when their vows would end and sacrifices would be offered for each of them. (Acts 21:26 NLT)

The Bible's historical account of Paul's Temple activities records that these sacrifices occurred *after* the resurrection of this alleged "fulfillment." This contradiction is often overlooked, but Paul engaged in Temple observance even after Yeshua's resurrection. The notion that Paul would write instructive letters as a rabbi condemning Temple practice while engaging in it himself should call into question Paul's character and authenticity. Paul either irrationally and publicly pursued that which he publicly condemned, or the mainstream has misunderstood what Paul wrote.

Another popular theory applied to dismantle Torah[1] (commonly translated as "the Law") observance for followers of Yeshua is that the very absence of a current operational Temple alone negates its importance after the miracle of a resurrected Messiah. This line of thinking becomes muddied when one considers the time of the first Temple destruction in 587 BCE. Afterward, there was no operational Temple for decades and no resurrected Messiah. The lack of a physical Temple did nothing to alter the reality of its significance pre-resurrection then, so its empirical physical existence has no bearing on its importance now. Still, this notion that the 1st Century

1. See BEKY Booklet, *What is the Torah?* by Hollisa Alewine

writings by Paul dismissed Temple relevance persists in the mainstream, and it is extended to include other Torah laws as well.

Designed as a companion text to *Colossal Controversies* and *Peter's Vision*, both by the author, *First Century Words Revealed to Twenty-First Century Believers* will illuminate the context and understanding of these letters from the historical and cultural perspective concurrent with the time frame in which they were written.

1

NOTHING REFUSED

Some of the more perplexing Ping Pong passages from these letters of antiquity only appear so because the authors were bound culturally to the Ancient Near East. Putting those letters into 1st Century cultural and religious context draws out the intentions of these letter-writers as they sought to promote the Word of the Lord.

The following is the proof text fueling the abolition of the dietary laws:

> Now the Spirit speaketh expressly, that in the latter times some shall depart from the faith, giving heed to seducing spirits, and doctrines of devils; 2 Speaking lies in hypocrisy; having their conscience seared with a hot iron; 3 Forbidding to marry, and commanding to abstain from foods, which God hath created to be received with thanksgiving of them

which believe and know the truth. 4 For every creature of Elohim is good, and nothing to be refused, if it be received with thanksgiving: 5 For it is sanctified by the word of Elohim and prayer. (1 Timothy 4:1-5 KJV)

Starting at a foundational level, interpretation of the letter to Timothy begins with understanding of the Rule of First Mention. This study concept is vital to divide truth accurately. The premise of this hermeneutical rule prescribes that how a word or topic is contextualized in the first mention of it remains consistent throughout the rest of the text. Secondly, the etymology of a word is paramount to understanding its meaning in the given passage at hand. This might sound altogether too simple, but given the fact that in most mainstream study circles this technique is not employed, learning it brings a new light and understanding of the Bible, even for those who have studied for decades. The etymology and Rule of First Mention are both interpretative techniques taught in Christian seminaries.

Many Bible translations compound this problem because they fail to consider the Hebrew texts. In addition, they plant words appropriate in a modern context, but they fail to convey what the Scripture meant in the original context. Discarding the original context is tantamount to rewriting the Bible. To increase palatability, sometimes Bible translators choose words to explain *an Eastern document through a Western lens*. Another shortcut is taking *verb-based Hebrew texts* and supplanting them with *noun-based Greek paradigms*. These techniques lead to dodging the accuracy and embracing the myth. The Hebrew Scriptures describe actions and reactions, while the Greek style of portrayal sinks into philosophical ideas. Facts and ideas are often worlds apart.

One example is the word "food." In Leviticus 11, God

goes into precise detail describing the characteristics of animals that may be eaten and animals that may not be eaten. He defines animals and creatures that are not to be consumed by human beings as "unclean," while He defines animals and creatures that may be consumed by people as "clean." After the lengthy and detailed descriptions of what may and may not be consumed, lest it be an abomination to Him (Lev 7:21), the Father repeats Himself.

> You must distinguish between the unclean and the clean, between living creatures that may be eaten and those that may not be eaten. (Lev 11:47 NIV)

Accepting that modern dispensational teachings dominate the mainstream,[2] one arrives at a very basic question.

> Q. Is an animal categorized as unclean by God to be defined as food?
>
> A. No. An animal described by the One Who created it as being unclean and not fit to be eaten by people is not food. Food means edible items.

Similarly, a cat is no more considered food than your dining room curtains. One might laugh off this example, but in many Bible versions, the chapter title added by the translators to break up chapters 10 and 11 in Leviticus reads: "Clean and Unclean Food." This title invention is misleading. It plants an idea that the inedible is edible *in theory*, but just not to God.

This approach suggests that the Creator may have an opinion about His creation, but that He lacks the ultimate authority to categorize its components

2. Dispensationalism is an interpretative method of the Bible employed by mainstream Christianity. Its tenets present biblical history as being divided into time frames viewed as "ages" where covenant terms fade in and out of relevance in progressive and regressive salience. This interpretation is challenged by many biblical scholars versed in the Hebrew and Greek languages.

regarding human consumption. The implication is that edible items are left to the discretion of the person. The person is part of the Creation, so this ultimately posits that the Creation interprets itself. "Clean and Unclean Food" as an added title is an oxymoron which sends a subtle message with an enormous impact on the view of God in sovereign relationship to His Creation.

Blurring the definition can lead people to forget that Creation was His work, not ours. People operate *within* Creation. They do not define it. There are only two categories of higher level beings that exist in intimate relationship; the Law Giver, and the law receivers. The Law Giver determines what is and what is not considered food within the law He gave. The law receiver may choose to obey or not, but there is no option of reassigning Creation based on his or her preference or desire. It is what it is. Belief or disbelief does not alter the empirical reality of what God assigns, says, and means.

In Scripture, God demarcates that which His people are to eat from that which they are to refrain from eating with a clear warning of the result.

> And the LORD God commanded the man, 'You are free to eat from any tree in the garden; but you must not eat from the tree of the knowledge of good and evil, for when you eat from it you will certainly die.' (Gen 2:16-17 NIV)

The forbidden tree contained death. Food is to nourish you, not to kill you. It is safe to say that the fruit of the tree of the knowledge of good and evil was not to be considered food to Adam and Eve, for they were instructed to refrain from eating it *lest they die.*

As for Eve, a dialogue with the serpent questions

their Creator's directive. Sometimes one question undermines that childlike faith. The result is that something so simple becomes complicated.

> Satan: "Has God indeed said, 'You shall not eat of every tree of the garden'?"
>
> Eve: "We may eat the fruit of the trees of the garden; 3 but of the fruit of the tree which is in the midst of the garden, God has said, 'You shall not eat it, nor shall you touch it, lest you die.'"
>
> Satan: "You will not surely die. 5 For God knows that in the day you eat of it your eyes will be opened, and you will be like God, knowing good and evil."

The result of this question ripples through our lives today.

> So when the woman saw that the tree was good for food, that it was pleasant to the eyes, and a tree desirable to make one wise, she took of its fruit and ate. She also gave to her husband with her, and he ate. 7 Then the eyes of both of them were opened, and they knew that they were naked, and they sewed fig leaves together and made themselves coverings. (Genesis 2: 7-7 NKJV)

How could something described as an item that would bring certain death upon it consumption be considered "good for food"? It couldn't. Through her sense and intellect, Eve reassigned an item God listed as "not food" to her list as "food."

What occurred?

- Eve listened to Satan question the commandment: "Did He REALLY say that?"
- She argued with the devil in defense: "We can't even touch it."
- Satan lied: "Do it. You won't really die."
- She interpreted benefit of the fruit from the forbidden tree with her own mind rather than through the commandments of God: "She saw that is was good for food" and reassigned it.
- They disobeyed the commandment.
- They were ashamed.

Just as Eve redefined what she considered to be food in alignment with her personal perspective, religious teachers sometime do the same, often unintentionally.

Returning to the Bible passage proof text listed earlier, what's evident is this *self-obedience* rather than *God-obedience* happens in the mainstream interpretation of the letter Paul wrote to Timothy.

> Now the Spirit speaketh expressly, that in the latter times some shall depart from the faith, giving heed to seducing spirits, and doctrines of devils;2 Speaking lies in hypocrisy; having their conscience seared with a hot iron; 3 Forbidding to marry, and commanding to abstain from foods, which God hath created to be received with thanksgiving of them which believe and know the truth. 4 For every creature of Elohim is good, and nothing to be refused, if it be received with thanksgiving: 5 For it is sanctified by the word of Elohim and prayer. (1 Timothy 4:1-5 KJV)

To be accurate in discerning exactly what this letter is conveying, some simplification of the text is necessary.

> **Q.** What items are being specifically described in the letter?
>
> "...commanding to abstain from foods, which God hath created to be received with thanksgiving of them which believe and know the truth."
>
> **A.** Food.

The word "food" in Greek used here is *broma*. Defined by Strong's G1033, broma is:

> A term used by Jews to speak of food. General food items allowed by Jewish Torah law.

This means clean items ONLY. The text identifies the explicit biblical description of what foods are referenced:

> ...which God hath created to be received by them which believe and know the truth.

These questions follow:

> **Q.** Where do we find what God "created to be received"?
>
> **A.** The Torah (Lev 11)
>
> **Q.** Received by whom?
>
> **A.** "by them which believe and know the truth"

Q. What is "the Truth"?

A. The Torah (Psalm 119:142)

This letter, when taken in proper context rather than modern cultural norms, discusses *clean items created by God to be eaten by believers who know the Torah*. This is simple enough, but without this contextual application, this letter is often promoted as evidence permitting the consumption of unclean items. Despite God having already forbidden such behavior in the Bible, this letter is deemed by some as an authoritative document that can override previous Scripture. This misunderstanding of the definition of food according to the Creator (Who does not change) makes accurately interpreting this letter impossible without adopting God's definitions. By knowing God's definition of food, His wisdom can be applied in study of this passage.

After applying the terms in this passage consistently with God's definitions, it's possible to plug in the contextually appropriate words that reveal the important message in this letter and the audience for whom it was intended.

> Now the Spirit speaketh expressly, that in the latter times some shall depart from the faith, giving heed to seducing spirits, and doctrines of devils; speaking lies in hypocrisy; having their conscience seared with a hot iron; forbidding to marry, and commanding to abstain from clean items, which God hath created to be received with thanksgiving by believers who know the Torah.

No ping-pong is going on in that verse anymore! Properly structuring and understanding even one sentence demonstrates the beautifully cohesive nature of the Father. He instructs according to His ways, not according to "dispensations of time" from which He as Eternal Creator of time is exempt. The entire message in the letter is consistent with every word which has proceeded out of the mouth of the Lord. As they would say in Jerusalem; Praise Hashem!

2

SEDUCING SPIRITS, LIES, AND HYPOCRISY

The letter to Timothy contains other curious designations: "Giving heed to seducing spirits."

Paul is describing a person (or persons) of whom to be wary. Are people who teach God's commandments as written in Leviticus and Deuteronomy "giving heed to seducing spirits" by doing so? If this letter is instructing believers to set aside the dietary laws, then by default, the teachers of the commandments *must* be the subject of this warning. If that is the case, Paul is accusing those who submit to the commandments of God to have been seduced into darkness by doing so. Not only that, they are striving to entice others into that "pit of obedience."

The irony in such an interpretation is palpable. Obedience to the commandments is not what puts believers at risk, disobedience does. Luring people into sin is the opposite of what Torah advocates are doing. The Bible instructs that steering humanity *toward the commandments* by example or education is the goal, not the temptation. The Ruach HaKodesh (Holy Spirit) that leads believers to obedience is not a "seducing spirit." All should avoid giving heed to seducing spirits, but learning from those who revere the commandments of God is not seduction to sin.

If this passage refers to the dietary laws, it represents the instruction of God's commandments in Leviticus and Deuteronomy as "a doctrine of devils." Are people who teach the biblical dietary laws verbatim from God's lips teaching "a doctrine of devils"? In other words, are God's words in the Torah *a doctrine of devils?*

> The law of the LORD is perfect, reviving the soul. The statutes of the LORD are trustworthy, making wise the simple. (Psalm 19:7 NIV)

The Bible which explicitly describes the Torah as perfect, reviving of the soul, and the source of wisdom, is now being labeled by Paul as a "doctrine of devils"? Talk about changing a definition! With this mindset, obeying the commandments is being posed as *a temptation from the devil*. One can start to comprehend how bizarre that is. Consider the image of the adversary trying to seduce people into obedience to God. It defies reason to picture the devil cunningly imploring; "Oh, come on. Obey the commandments. It will be great!"

"Torah is my favorite. Use it just the way He commanded.
Learn it and teach it to your children and your children's children."

As students consider that improbability, it's prudent to ask a related question. What truly is a "doctrine of the devil"?

> "Go ahead. EAT IT! He said not to,
> BUT YOU CAN!"

Frighteningly, that evil doctrine of the serpent sums up and matches the erroneous interpretation of this letter! The adversary seeks to steal, kill and destroy. From the very beginning, Satan didn't tempt mankind to *obey the law*. He tempts mankind to *disobey it*. In obedience to God's holy Word, there is life. In disobedience to His word is death. Open rebellion is a deadly game in one way or another. No exceptions.

> You will again obey the Lord and
> follow all his commands I am giving
> you today. Then the Lord your God
> will make you most prosperous in all
> the work of your hands and in the

> fruit of your womb, the young of your livestock and the crops of your land. The Lord will again delight in you and make you prosperous, just as he delighted in your fathers, if you obey the Lord your God and keep his commands and decrees that are written in this Book of the Law and turn to the Lord your God with all your heart and with all your soul. (Deuteronomy 30:8-10 NIV)

Wouldn't the Evil One like believers in Yeshua to have that backward?

> This day I call heaven and earth as witnesses against you that I have set before you life and death, blessings and curses. Now choose life, so that you and your children may live. (Deuteronomy 30:19 NIV)

The Timothy letter further describes the teachers in question as "speaking lies in hypocrisy."

This classification could not apply to those instructing God's commandments. Are those teaching obedience to God's laws speaking lies in hypocrisy? We have already identified God's laws as THE TRUTH according to the Bible. Now it's "lies"? What about the next descriptor of "forbidding to marry"? This does that apply to the Torah-observant follower of Yeshua either. Nowhere in the Word does one read that he or she is commanded not to marry. In fact, the commandment is just the opposite, all of Scripture presumes marriage. These things are not taught by anyone who is teaching God's law. Paul is *not* speaking of those teaching observance to the Torah dietary laws. None of those classifications can be attributed to a Torah promoter because those things do not describe anything in the Torah.

The obvious need for a deeper understanding of this letter is likely forming in a student's mind. A student who never read this letter in context might be surprised at how removed the mainstream is from applying logical study methods when reading these letters. However, if it seems unimaginable that so many to have it so wrong for so long, have no fear. The Bible speaks the truth. The truth can't hurt people. The truth can only set people free. No one should hold onto errors just because they have invested in unknowingly making them. The student can step out and be free. Be encouraged. These are the days of Elijah. Elijah was the Northern Kingdom Prophet who performed miracles to beckon those of the covenant back to the Torah. (1 Kings 17-19)

> Remember the law of my servant Moses, the statutes and rules that I commanded him at Horeb for all Israel. Behold, I will send you Elijah the Prophet before the great and awesome day of the LORD comes. (Malachi 4:4-5 ESV)

There is little dispute that time is blazing by and prophecy is being realized in our day. If you are learning something "new" in this current age that was not in the mainstream in days past, fear not. This "new" information is a *return* to that which was never expired, but forgotten.

.

3

RECEIVED WITH THANKSGIVING

In Verse Four of the letter to Timothy, a passage is often plucked out and treated as a stand-alone passage to justify eating unclean things.

> For every creature of Elohim is good, and nothing to be refused, if it be received with thanksgiving: for it is sanctified by the word of Elohim and prayer.

When this verse is isolated and taken out of context, a common assumption is that we are commanded by Paul to eat swine flesh, rats, or other unclean items "with thanksgiving." What is the realistic probability of that? First, does Paul have the authority to command or permit actions that Heaven forbids? [3] Second, if God forbade unclean animals (and it is written that He did), why would anyone thank Him while he or she ate it? He didn't provide it. Quite the contrary, He denies His people the opportunity to do so. There was no mincing of words, no nebulous

3. See BEKY Booklet, *Peter's Vision: Beacon or Bacon?* by the author.

sentences that could be interpreted in various ways. All that is seen are the clear-cut instructions of what is to be considered food and what is not.

Is Paul, who asserted that the Torah was holy to the Romans (Romans 7:12), now suggesting to Timothy that it is to be pushed aside on matters of food? Paul has no authority to bestow upon Timothy a new Divine superpower invoked by human gratitude. When applied to animals, this imagined superpower does not miraculously alter the classification God assigned for it. Neither Timothy nor any other Torah student, pastor, or rabbi possesses that power. If God declares unclean animals as an abomination to eat, how brazen is Paul to suggest a way around this reality? Human mortal appreciation is not influential enough to make the unclean creature clean. Thankfulness does not dismiss the dietary laws.

There is no catch-all answer that washes God's spiritual, holy, and life-giving teachings down one unexamined, unfiltered drain such as *"Jesus made it clean."* Paul does *not* say that things that were declared by the Creator as unclean are now clean because the Messiah said so *anywhere in the entire Bible*, let alone in this letter. The bacon advocate will often move to provide a generalized dispensational theology devoid of details or evidence. Bible study cannot *bypass the details* of the content to operate in abstractions. That is the trick of the politician, not the method of the scholar. A politician can't answer the actual question, so he proposes a pseudo-parallel idea with a manufactured resolution, hoping the masses don't notice.

If it is true that Jesus declared all unclean things clean, why didn't Paul just plainly say that the Messiah said this? Unhinging thousands of years of dietary practice by Israelite believers would be HUGE for anyone to suggest, let alone be taken seriously. Quoting the Messiah on this topic would be the vital piece of evidence. Being blunt and direct on such an enormous undertaking is mandatory.

Power has been ascribed to Paul's letters by many Christian denominations which supplants the power of what God has written as commandments, despite the fact that these commandments were given for *all generations*. Given that this is a letter written by mortal Paul, (who is a "he" with a lowercase h) writing to new believers, Paul has been almost deified mass obedience to his alleged countermand of God's Word. Paul himself could not define truth by declaring; "I know this is truth even though it competes with what has been written by God because I wrote it in a letter last month." Paul did not create truth, add to it, nor take away from the words of the Scriptures. Paul was a Torah scholar of scholars (Acts 22:3). He lived by the Torah as His source of truth, never denied it was the truth, and would never consider suggesting any of it irrelevant. Proclaiming that he did so would not please Paul. Circumventing the commandments was not what Paul was commissioned to do, nor did he ever do so.

4

FULFILLED BY THE RESURRECTION

Some theologians hint that Paul wasn't proposing that the commandments are now *irrelevant* post-Calvary, but were *"fulfilled"* by the Messiah through His death and resurrection, and it was upon *this* authority that the dietary laws are no longer required. Is "no longer required" akin to "irrelevant"? Challenge yourself and attempt to dispute that these mean the same thing. It's a tough one! Since this perception of the law being "fulfilled" casts a doubtful shadow, a short detour is necessary to examine Paul's words.

The words allegedly uttered by Jesus that He made "all things clean" are suggested to have been in effect *the moment they were declared*, and they were declared *prior to His resurrection*. If one is using this example as evidence of a resurrected fulfillment, the argument collapses upon itself by the timing and setting of the alleged declaration.

Consider Matthew's record of Jesus stating that He had come to fulfill the law.

> Do not think that I have come to
> abolish the Law or the Prophets; I
> have not come to abolish them but
> to fulfill them. (Matthew 5:17 NIV)

The Messiah assures His disciples that He came not to abolish the Law or the Prophets, but to fulfill them. The word translated as "fulfill" is Strong's G4136 *pleroo*. This is defined as "fill, complete, or fully teach/preach." The word translated as "abolish" is Strong's G2647, *kataluó*. Kataluo is defined as "destroy, overthrow, break up, unharness a carriage horse or pack animal, loosen, unyoke."

For context, compare this use of pleroo with another usage in which Paul uses this word to refer to himself.

> ...by the power of signs and
> wonders, through the power of the
> Spirit of God. So from Jerusalem all
> the way around to Illyricum, I have
> fully proclaimed the gospel of Christ.
> (Romans 15:19 NIV)

If pleroo is translated consistently with the usage of "fulfill" in Matthew's account, the question arises about what it means when *Paul claims to have fulfilled the gospel*. In other translations, this word pleroo is translated as "presented," "proclaimed," or "preached." Paul uses that word regarding himself in *his personal ministry* again:

> I have become its servant by the
> commission God gave me to present
> to you the word of God in its fullness.
> (Colossians 1:25 NIV)

The word "fulfill" in Greek does not mean what it is often perceived to mean in English, *or* Paul is calling *himself* the completion of the work of the Messiah, rather than what the Messiah Himself stated when He said it was "finished." (John 19:30)

The Messiah did not need Paul to complete His ministry, but rather to share the completed details of it to the sheep.[4] Without the context of words and their usage, the reader cannot understand, but with these tools, simple reminders like this become unnecessary.

The next verses give context to what Messiah said in Matthew's gospel give fuller context:

> For truly I tell you, until heaven and earth disappear, not the smallest letter, not the least stroke of a pen, will by any means disappear from the Law until everything is accomplished. Therefore, anyone who sets aside one of the least of these commands and teaches others accordingly will be called least in the kingdom of heaven, but whoever practices and teaches these commands will be called great in the kingdom of heaven. (Matthew 5:18-19)

It makes absolute sense contextually with the Truth already revealed in the Bible about the Law when the word "pleroo" is translated as "preach" or "fully teach." "Abolish" means to relax or loosen. Inserting the proper understanding of the words in focus reads logically.

> Do not think that I have come [to relax] the Law or the Prophets; I have not come to abolish them but [to preach] them. For truly I tell you, until heaven and earth disappear, not the smallest letter, not the least stroke of a pen, will by any means disappear from the Law until everything is accomplished. Therefore anyone who sets aside

4. See the author's BEKY Booklet, *Divorce and Remarriage in the Bible*.

> one of the least of these commands and teaches others accordingly will be called least in the kingdom of heaven, but whoever practices and teaches these commands will be called great in the kingdom of heaven. (Matthew 5:17-19)

Yeshua preaches that which He asserts is a permanent earthly fixture of practice. Our Messiah was the greatest Rabbi, Teacher, and Counselor ever to walk the planet. He declares that He came to preach and teach that which He deems as binding and vital until Heaven and Earth pass away and ALL is accomplished. Yeshua even declares that anyone relaxing *even the least of the laws* is to be considered least in the Kingdom. The far stretch is to believe is that He bounces back and forth in a single conversation between stating the significance of the law, His mission NOT to abolish it, and the reduction in status of those who would even suggest to loosen them slightly, to *fully loosening it Himself because He obeyed it.*

We are to walk as He walked, and He walked out the Torah "fulfilling" it, the point becomes even sharper. We are to walk out the commandments to "fulfill" them too. If that's what He did, then that is what we are to do. It should come as a relief to know that the Bible is a wonderful, cohesive document that can be trusted in its consistent flow of truth.

5

SANCTIFIED FOOD

> Irony regards every simple truth as a challenge. ~ Mason Cooley

Messiah did not lift, or even loosen the dietary laws. The letter from Paul to Timothy has context in "sanctified" foods. Amazingly, there is still more content in this letter where logic was neglected:

> For every creature of Elohim is good, and nothing to be refused, if it be received with thanksgiving: for it is sanctified by the word of Elohim and prayer.

The word "sanctified" is *hagiazó*, Strong's G37:

hagiazo - set apart, make holy, consecrate

Reading this verse from the perspective that our gratitude transforms the inedible unclean to edible clean doesn't even make sense in the sentence. The text states that God, by His Word, "set apart" animals. What does this mean? It means *that by His word He set apart animals that are meant for food*. With this "setting apart," He provided the means to identify them in their status by His detailed descriptions of their characteristics. *He defined that.* His people did not, nor could they ever. Thus, the animals He sanctified as food by His Word, no one may suggest cannot be eaten.

If all animals are now clean by personal gratitude, then, how can any of them be defined as "animals set apart"? Set apart from what? That erroneous interpretation renders animals all one homogenized group, which leaves no possibility of anything being set apart. That makes no sense. "Set apart" does not mean "the same." How can they be "set apart" and "not set apart" simultaneously? They can't. Anything "sanctified by the word of God" is sealed in the designated status God gave it in His Word.

The passage also cannot mean that all creatures are set apart as food for people, for one bite of a poisonous dart frog will stop a human heart within three minutes. The same goes for the Puffer Fish, the Marbled Cone Snail, and the Blue-ringed Octopus, just to name a few. The creatures that were set apart by God for human consumption are sanctified by His Word: set apart for a specific purpose by His description. The Dart Frog has a purpose in the ecosystem, but all agree that its purpose is not to sit on a dinner plate.

Ultimately, the word of God is the final say, regardless of what man says. If God says a particular meat is permissible, then it is permissible. His Word is defines everything. After all, He created everything! If He says it is unclean in Leviticus 11 and Deuteronomy 14, isn't that true? Change is nonnegotiable despite the wave of baconism experienced today.

Try reading this entire passage again:

> In the latter times some shall depart from the faith, giving heed to seducing spirits, and doctrines of devils; speaking lies in hypocrisy; having their conscience seared with a hot iron; forbidding to marry, and commanding to abstain from meats, which God hath created to be received with thanksgiving by those which believe and know the truth.

The passage in this letter is not talking about the dietary laws at all. In fact, the dietary laws are not even mentioned.

1. Torah is not a doctrine of devils. It's just the opposite.
2. The Torah is not "lies in hypocrisy." It's just the opposite.
3. Torah does not forbid marriage. It does just the opposite.
4. Torah does not forbid eating things created to be received as food. It does just the opposite.

What could be suggested as the source of faulty doctrine? The following offers a hint:

> We frankly say, yes, the Roman Catholic Church made this change, made this law, as she made many other laws, for instance, the Friday abstinence (no meat of any kind allowed on Friday), the unmarried priesthood, the laws concerning mixed marriages, the regulation of Catholic marriages and a thousand other laws. (Kraemer, 1975)

Here many of these descriptives are accounted

for in one religious system. Kraemer's statement provokes thought. The syncretic Roman doctrine was popular in the region of the audience during the time contemporary to the letter. The 1st Century doctrine:

1. forbade marital unions of those in religious service
2. forbade the consumption of clean meats on certain days
3. diverted from other laws by replacement holidays, etc. unabashedly

These digressions from the written Word would be considered a doctrine of the devil and lies in hypocrisy by Yeshua's disciples, and they would have disputed any alterations made to the Word. Yes, this suggestion is controversial. Can open, worms everywhere. This proposal might be difficult to tolerate, but it is a valid proposition.

The irony of how these letters are read in the

mainstream and what is actually in them is striking. These passages written to Timothy are not saying that people can alter the status of something unclean and render it clean with attitudes or words. *Paul is saying that no one can alter the status of clean, thus rendering it unclean with their words or attitudes.* God, not people, does the sanctifying. People establish nothing. They are instructed to thank Him for what He has established and go with it. These letters aren't warning about people teaching others to honor God's law. Paul here is warning about the people who teach another doctrine of man's authority that alters, circumvents, or dismisses any part of God's law. Jesus gave them this answer:

> Very truly I tell you, the Son can do nothing by himself; he can do only what he sees his Father doing, because whatever the Father does the Son also does. (John 5:19 NIV)

God's law says that He created meats/foods that are set apart as permissible, and He is the only one who can call His creation permissible for eating or not. Man has no authority over what God has sanctified, regardless of our gratitude or prayer. All the people are called to do is trust Him, obey Him, and be thankful.

6

WHAT GOES IN, OR WHAT COMES OUT?

In earlier chapters, this booklet mentioned the topic of the Messiah discussing clean and unclean things in Mark's gospel. The Gospel of Mark is another place where verse plucking augmented a theology which discards the dietary laws.

> The Pharisees and some of the teachers of the law who had come from Jerusalem gathered around Jesus and saw some of his disciples eating food with hands that were defiled, that is, unwashed. (The Pharisees and all the Jews do not eat unless they give their hands a ceremonial washing, holding to the tradition of the elders. When they come from the marketplace they do not eat unless they wash. And they observe many other traditions,

such as the washing of cups, pitchers and kettles). So the Pharisees and teachers of the law asked Jesus, 'Why don't your disciples live according to the tradition of the elders instead of eating their food with defiled hands?' "He replied, "'Isaiah was right when he prophesied about you hypocrites; as it is written:

These people honor me with their lips, but their hearts are far from me. They worship me in vain; their teachings are merely human rules. You have let go of the commands of God and are holding on to human traditions.'"

And he continued, "'You have a fine way of setting aside the commands of God in order to observe your own traditions! For Moses said,

Honor your father and mother and anyone who curses their father or mother is to be put to death.

But you say that if anyone declares that what might have been used to help their father or mother is korban (that is, devoted to God) then you no longer let them do anything for their father or mother. Thus you nullify the word of God by your tradition that you have handed down. And you do many things like that.'" Again Jesus called the crowd to him and said, 'Listen to me, everyone, and understand this. Nothing outside a person can defile them by going into them. Rather, it is what comes out of a person that defiles them.' After he had left the crowd and entered the house, his disciples asked him about this parable. 'Are you so dull?' he asked. 'Don't you see that nothing that enters a person from the outside can defile them? For it doesn't go into their heart but into their stomach, and then out of the body.' (In saying this, Jesus declared all foods clean.) He went on: 'What comes out of a person is what defiles them. For it is from within, out of a person's heart, that evil thoughts come—sexual immorality, theft, murder, adultery, greed, malice, deceit, lewdness, envy, slander, arrogance and folly. All these evils come from inside and defile a person.' (Mark 7:1-23 NIV)

Yeshua was a Jewish rabbi (teacher). If He had undermined any Torah commandments, He would have been instantly stripped of His credentials and executed. That was the method of dealing with such blatant heresy during that time. An argument would not ensue, a mortal punishment would. Messiah was never found to be guilty of anything, much less speaking against the most basic commandments of God. The dietary laws during by this time remained an unchallenged cultural and Scriptural norm, and they were not a controversial topic as they now are in modern Christianity.

Secondly, look at this comment the Messiah makes:

> Nothing outside a person can defile them by going into them.

The word "nothing" Yeshua uses is Strong's G3762 *oudeís*:

> No one, nothing at all - a powerful negating conjunction.
>
> Oudeis rules out by definition objectively without exception, is deductive in force so it excludes every (any) example that is included within the premise (supposition), ("not one, none") categorically excludes, declaring as a fact that no valid example exists.

In essence, if the Messiah was discussing eating, He is declaring that there is *absolutely nothing on the outside that can defile a person if eaten*. Nothing. Remember the poisonous dart frog? Turn your thoughts to a hot mug of bleach, snake venom, or murky pond water. Even consider a 1350 calorie fast food breakfast that has 65 grams of fat. Can that defile a body? Is it reasonable to state that none of these things can cause harm or detriment to the body? Considering the word the Messiah used, there is no wiggle room to interpret.

People often latch onto several sentences in the midst of these verses, focusing on vs 17-23:

> Don't you see that nothing that enters a person from the outside can defile them? For it doesn't go into their heart but into their stomach, and then out of the body." (In saying this, Jesus declared all foods clean.) He went on: 'What comes out of a person is what defiles them. For it is from within, out of a person's heart, that evil thoughts come—sexual immorality, theft, murder, adultery, greed, malice, deceit, lewdness, envy, slander, arrogance and folly. All these evils come from inside and defile a person.' (Mark 7:17-23 NIV)

When read as a stand-alone point, it can appear as if the Messiah was changing the commandments by striking the dietary laws set by His Father. While these actions go against everything He ever said He would do, has done, or was commissioned to do, many teachers have persisted in taking the verbiage out of context and marking these 1st Century letters as the final say on all matters.

To discover the message the Messiah was teaching, it's vital to establish context to the words the Messiah was speaking by reading earlier in the letter.

> Now when the Pharisees gathered to him, with some of the scribes who had come from Jerusalem, they saw that some of his disciples ate with hands that were defiled, that is, unwashed. (For the Pharisees and all the Jews do not eat unless they wash their hands properly, holding to the tradition of the elders, and when they come from the marketplace, they do not eat unless they wash and there are many other traditions that they observe, such as the washing of cups and pots and copper vessels and dining couches). And the Pharisees and the scribes asked him, 'Why do your disciples not walk according to the tradition of the elders, but eat with defiled hands?' (Mark 7:1-5 NIV)

Asking the most basic question reveals a simple, logical answer:

> **Q.** What was the topic of the Pharisees to which the Messiah was responding?
>
> **A.** The topic was unwashed hands.

Meat wasn't mentioned at all. The dietary laws were not addressed at any point in this letter. The Pharisees asked Yeshua why His followers were not engaging in traditional ritual hand washing before they ate bread. Notice they did not question Yeshua's behavior on the matter, so evidently, the Messiah did do the hand washing blessing before He ate His bread as is the tradition in the Mishnah.[5] Their interrogation was focused on His disciples.

Context brings along with it a companion known as logic. When these documents are approached rationally, they arrive like friends bringing hot (and kosher) chicken soup on a cold day. The topic is ritually unwashed hands. For those dining enjoying a big ham served alongside crockpots full of pork and beans, the topic in this letter might be viewed as a mandate to dismantle the dietary laws, but there is no evidence for that anywhere in this letter. The Pharisees did not ask Yeshua why His followers were eating unclean animals, but rather, they asked: "Why do Your disciples not walk according to the tradition of the elders, but eat bread with unwashed hands?"

The action in question by the Pharisees is not about the Torah's dietary laws regarding what meat is permissible to eat, so there is no reason to insert this text into a bacon advocating argument, and yet it is one of the most popular rationales to hanging onto that BLT. The Pharisees are speaking about the tradition of the elders, which is described in Talmudic ritual handwashing instructions:

> Before washing your hands, be sure that they are clean and free of anything that will obstruct the waters from reaching the entire surface of your hands. This is a spiritual experience, you recall. Remove your rings—unless you never remove them, in which case they are considered "part of your hand." Fill

5. See BEKY Booklet, Introduction to the Jewish Sources by S. Creeger.

a cup with water and pour twice on your right hand. Repeat on the left. (Lefties: reverse the order.) Pour three times on each hand. Make sure the water covers your entire hand until the wrist bone with each pour. Separate your fingers slightly to allow the water in between them. After washing, lift your hands chest-high and say:

Blessed are you, L-rd our G-d, King of the universe, who has sanctified us with His commandments, and commanded us concerning the washing of the hands.

[Say this blessing only if you intend to eat more than two ounces of bread.] Rub your hands together and then dry them. Be careful not to speak or get involved in anything else until you've recited the blessing on your bread and swallowed some too. If you take a washroom break during your meal, or otherwise soil your hands, you need to wash again—this time, without a blessing. (Shulhan Aruk Orach Chaim 158:1)

What is the word used for what was eaten with unwashed hands?

> Then the Pharisees and scribes asked Him, 'Why do Your disciples not walk according to the tradition of the elders, but eat bread (Greek arton) with unwashed hands?' (Mark 7:5-6)

Basic question, basic answer:

Q. What were they eating?

A. Bread.

The food eaten was bread. If that's the case (and it is) then why would it be supposed Yeshua is talking about meat? If meat is not involved, then why use this verse in the discussion of what meats may or may not be eaten? The answer to that is the theme which keeps resurfacing. Most people never really investigate the words of this letter. Rather, they rely on the impression of the letter taught by those who promote a dispensational theology that clashes with the Bible, causing the Bible to appear like two competing volumes of warring deities. It becomes understandable why any faithful Jew would question a Messiah who has been depicted so incorrectly.

What creature outside the dietary laws could potentially relate to unwashed bread-eating hands? The simple answer is nothing. There is not the slightest chance that on a kosher Jewish table that unclean meat could be found on those bread-eating unwashed hands. The only reasonable assumption even to a student not familiar with the Talmud [6] is that dirt was on those unwashed hands. So logically, meat is simply "off the table" (forgive the pun) in this passage, as there is no reference to it, nor is there any hint to meat at all.

6. See BEKY Booklet, *Introduction to the Jewish Sources* by S. Creeger.

7. See BEKY Booklet, *Truth, Tradition or Tare* by Hollisa Alewine.

Further, Messiah isn't even talking about dirt! He is talking about the good traditions of the elders that were being enforced while the weightier matters of the commandments of God (love, justice, and mercy) were being neglected.[7] Those repudiating His followers for not ritually handwashing were the local hypocrites in their behavior toward mankind, thus having "dirty hands" themselves despite their ritual hand washing.

These particular Pharisees were aggressively condemning their guests for neglecting Jewish tradition while they violated the actual Torah commandments themselves. In doing so, this was an act of shaming their guests with embarrassment, which is a more significant violation of the laws and customs. The *Pirkei Avot*,[8] a traditional section of Jewish law, demands hospitable treatment of other human beings. Yeshua embraced the traditions, but He had perfect graded wisdom. He knew the hierarchy of how the written Word and traditions were to be ordered and applied. Our ultimate Teacher leads us in observance as any good Rabbi should.

How did Yeshua answer the complaint of the religious leaders?

> He answered and said to them, 'Well did Isaiah prophesy of you hypocrites, as it is written: "'This people honors Me with their lips, but their heart is far from Me. And in vain they worship Me, teaching as doctrines the commandments of men.'"
>
> For laying aside the commandment of God, you hold the tradition of men—the washing of pitchers and cups, and many other such things you do.' He said to them, 'All too well you reject the commandment of God, that you may keep your tradition.' (Mark 7:8-9)

Yeshua isn't even talking about hands, meat, or even bread for that matter. While food has been the focus applied to these comments, the most beautiful point that Yeshua makes is sidestepped. He is talking about our hearts in obedience to the commandments, not giving a free pass to dismiss some of them. Messiah is

8. "Ethics of the Fathers"

not questioning the dietary laws. The dietary laws are commandments of God. He is rebuking the religious leaders who were judging their guests on an outward tradition while tolerating in themselves the foul fruit of their hypocritical lives. This sort of leadership harms communities and individuals, and Yeshua spoke out against it.

Yeshua continues:

> For Moses said, 'Honor your father and your mother'; and, 'He who curses father or mother, let him be put to death.' But you say, 'If a man says to his father or mother, "'Whatever profit you might have received from me is Korban...'"
> (Mark 7:10-13)

Sometimes this is interpreted that Yeshua was against the traditions of the elders. There is no reason to believe Yeshua carried an anti-tradition bias whatsoever. When these traditions were used as a platform for men to exert cutting authority over other men while the perpetrators refused to live in the weightier matters of justice and mercy, Yeshua reacted strongly in grace for the sake of the community for whom these men were shepherds. It would not be unreasonable to assume that during a private moment with the disciples involved He did reprimand them for not performing the bread blessing and hand washing, but during this meal and in the presence of malicious hearts, He was focused on the hypocrisy of the elders above the neglect of His followers.

Two opposite points are contrasted here:

What Jesus said:	A new idea:
"...making the Word of God of no effect through your tradition."	"Set aside what has been written, for here is a new way for you to live."

How is what Yeshua was concerned about, which was: "do not budge on what the Father has decreed for you to do in favor of tradition" now interpreted as "forget those decrees, I have a new tradition of eating for everyone now"? The words He truly spoke and the modern anti-Torah interpretation are opposed each other. Many consciences have been seared with a hot iron, yet Messiah is asking us *to listen.*

> When He had called all the multitude to Himself, He said to them, 'Hear Me, everyone, and understand: There is nothing that enters a man from outside which can defile him; but the things which come out of him, those are the things that defile a man. If anyone has ears to hear, let him hear!' (Mark 7:14-16)

Here is a paraphrase:

Whatever is on ritually unwashed hands that gets into your body when you are eating bread should not cause you to regard that bread or those hands as unclean. The actions of your hardened hearts should be of great alarm to you, as this is what causes spiritual ill health and destruction.

When His followers mentioned the offense taken by the leaders, Yeshua illustrates this destruction and the need for Him to rebuke them publicly for the sake of the people with a parable.

> Then the disciples came to him and asked, 'Do you know that the Pharisees were offended when they heard this?' He replied, 'Every plant that my heavenly Father has not planted will be pulled up by the roots. Leave them; they are blind guides. If the blind lead the blind, both will fall into a pit.' Peter said, 'Explain the parable to us.' 'Are you still so dull?' Jesus asked them. 'Don't you see that whatever enters the mouth goes into the stomach and then out of the body? But the things that come out of a person's mouth come from the heart, and these defile them. For out of the heart come evil thoughts—murder, adultery, sexual immorality, theft, false testimony, slander. These are what defile a person; but eating with unwashed hands does not defile them.' (Matthew 10:12-20 NIV)

In Mark's account, more of the story is reported:

> When He had entered a house away from the crowd, His disciples asked Him concerning the parable. So, He said to them, 'Are you thus without understanding also? Do you not perceive that whatever enters a man from outside cannot defile him, because it does not enter his heart but his stomach, and is eliminated? (Thus purifying all foods)?' (Mark 7:17-23 NIV)

NEWS FLASH!

That last tag line in parenthesis in most translations

"Thus purifying all foods"

is not in the original Greek text. This was added by the translators.

However, *even if it was in the original text*, it is translated improperly from the inserted Greek into English. The word is not "purify" in this context at all. In context with the word "eliminated" the word is "purge":

Kathartos

Strong's G2511 defined as "to cleanse, to purge, to purify"

"Purge" fits with the prior word "eliminated" while "purify" does not. The word translated as "purifying" in verse 19 is only contextually accurate when translated as "purge," when something is eliminated. That which is eliminated is not "purified." It is PURGED. This understanding does not require any more knowledge than basic "Going to The Bathroom 101."

Another question and answer for perspective:

> **Q.** What were the metaphoric "impure" elements here?
>
> **A.** Uncleanness on "ritually unwashed," but otherwise clean, hands. The pure part is extracted and the impure part is eliminated (purged).

Never has it been taught in any anatomy class that what is eliminated is purified. The translators thought that could help the reader out, but the scientific evidence of e. *coli, cyclosporiasis,* and other infections and diseases caused by contact with human waste defy the clean outhouse doctrine.

> Do you not perceive that whatever enters a man from outside cannot defile him, because it does not enter his heart but his stomach, and is eliminated (thus purging all foods)?

When comparing Ping Pong translations of this

added text, additional thorny roadblocks appear. Some of the modern translations have altered these words "thus purifying all foods" altogether, completely reconstructing the meaning. Compare some common translations.

> For it doesn't go into their heart but into their stomach, and then out of the body. (In saying this, Jesus declared all foods clean.) (NIV)

> Food doesn't go into your heart, but only passes through the stomach and then goes into the sewer. (By saying this, he declared that every kind of food is acceptable in God's eyes.) (NLT)

> Since it enters not his heart but his stomach, and is expelled? (Thus he declared all foods clean.) (ESV)

There are some significant differences here. Interesting![9]

> **Q.** What about the word THUS as used in the ESV? Is this in the original manuscript?
>
> **A.** No

With an added "thus" and a removed "the," the text reads:

> Do you not understand that whatever goes into the man from outside cannot defile him, because it does not enter his heart but into his stomach, and is eliminated (thus He declared all food clean) .(Mark 7:18-19 ESV).

9. See Appendix A.

In this translation, the translators ADDED

1. Thus
2. Jesus
3. Declared
4. Clean

With no added or removed words it reads:

> Do you not perceive that whatever goes into the man from outside cannot defile him, because it does not enter his heart but into his stomach, and is eliminated, purging all the foods?

In their translation, translators REMOVED

1. purged

The translators added to and removed from the Word. The opposite of what was written was printed in the Bible.

The topic was religious leaders shaming the disciples by harping on a hand-washing tradition while they heartlessly transgressed humanitarian commandments to the detriment of the flock. Taking the words out of the context suggests that the Messiah is changing the Word of God (which disqualifies Him as being the Messiah), and....

THERE IS NOTHING THAT CAN HURT YOU?

By this reasoning, people can safely:

- Eat roadkill
- Drink Clorox
- Drink blood
- Take drugs
- Eat human flesh
- Eat puffer fish
- Eat meats REPEATEDLY deemed as unclean for food by God

By this rationale, Isaiah's words about this future event must be discarded:

> 'Those who sanctify themselves and purify themselves, to go to the gardens. After an idol in the midst, eating swine's flesh and the abomination and the mouse, shall be consumed together,' says the LORD. 'For I know their works and their thoughts. It shall be that I will

> gather all nations and tongues; and they shall come and see My glory.'
> (Isaiah 66:17)

Was Yeshua going against what His Father commanded or going against what the Pharisees were doing? What is more likely?

    a.   The Messiah was correcting the Torah

    b.   The Messiah was correcting the Pharisees.

Here, severe irony lurks. This passage revealing Messiah's disgust that men were ignoring the commandments of the Torah, is used to justify disobeying the Torah. This verse is being used to rationalize breaking Torah when Yeshua is specifically teaching is that it is wrong to lay Torah aside.

Even further, the Pharisees did not accuse Yeshua of eating unclean meat; they admonished His followers for not washing their hands before they ate bread. Messiah was furious that the leadership cared more about an easy, outwardly pious tradition above the inward heart commandments. Yeshua did not change the Torah status of meat that lies within a perfect, unchangeable Law that He promised He did not come to abolish. The translators' suggestion is that *the Messiah is accusing the Pharisees of elevating the Word of God above being a good person.* Let *that* sink in. Isn't the Word of God how we learn to be a good person?

Yeshua the Messiah would not say, "Torah shmorah. I would rather you just be nice." Yeshua did just the opposite. He is rightfully accusing the privileged beacons of the Father of putting a nice outward tradition above the more difficult, character commandments. He appropriately exposes the religious hypocrisy thrust upon the community.

As always, the Messiah was furious that the

commandments were not being kept by the community role models. This is not the Messiah saying; "Forget the dietary commandments. Concentrate on other ways of behaving well instead." He is saying; "Live in My ways of justice and mercy first, and then your outward traditions can be beneficial." Yeshua mentions the commandment of honoring your father and mother had been supplanted, replacing that observance with offering that resource to the Temple rather than to the parents. This rendered the commandment to honor parents ineffective. The former is done in private and is a way of living for community harmony and brotherly love, while the latter is a public presentation of a gift neglects the weightier commandment. Handwashing traditions, gifts, and offerings are all good things to do, but not when the inner man decays with spiritual rot. First things first.

If Yeshua said, "Go ahead. Eat animals without a cloven hoof and that do not chew their cud," He would be least in the Kingdom of Heaven. Matthew 5:17 quotes Yeshua saying; "Whoever lays aside even the smallest commandment and teaches others to do so will be least in the Kingdom of Heaven."

The Pharisees, who were doing anything they could to discredit claims of Yeshua being the Messiah, never one time accused Yeshua or any of His followers of breaking the dietary laws. That's because He never gave them a reason to! He never broke them!

> The chief priests and the whole Sanhedrin were looking for evidence against Yeshua so that they could put him to death, but they did not find any. (Mark 14:55 NIV)

In these letters meat is not even mentioned. The Word of God states that bread is clean, even without hand-washing rituals. The point of the handwashing ritual is to demonstrate a clean and thankful heart before God. This tradition encourages, edifies, and should be honored when possible, but there are weightier matters.

This letter is not challenging the uncleanness of unclean meats, but rather it is challenging uncleanness of man eating bread with ritually washed hands in stiff-necked rebellion to what is truly good. If a flock is being led by the hard-hearted, even the simple traditions meant to foster a cohesive community can become a burden.

CONCLUSION

The Word of God states that pork and shellfish are unclean. That has not changed. If unclean animals were made clean by Yeshua in this letter in the New Testament, then how can there be unclean birds in Revelation, which speaks of the future?

> With a mighty voice he shouted: 'Fallen! Fallen is Babylon the Great! She has become a dwelling for demons and a haunt for every impure spirit, a haunt for every unclean bird, a haunt for every unclean and detestable animal.' (Revelation 18:2 NIV)

Delving deeply into the original words as they were written in these apostolic letters and Gospel accounts, establishing context, applying the Rule of First Mention, and trusting the Word of God upholds the Torah. These passages do not dismiss the dietary laws, but rather affirm them as precious instructions from a Father to His beloved children. As a parent, He guides those whom He loves in His ways, and each time His beloved are faced with a meal choice, we can feel His Fatherly hand pressing on our shoulders with instruction, love, and care. This is sanctification.

Paul, Timothy, and Mark were petitioners of purity, not partners in crime. The honor was theirs. The relief is ours. We can rest in His Word and trust His precept. We can know that we are handled with care and given identity in Him. Like the Patriarch Jacob, disciples of Yeshua are given a new way to walk, never to walk the same way again.

Q. How can a BLT ever compete with that kind of love?

A. It can't.

Shalom!

QUESTIONS FOR REVIEW

1. Is it recorded in scripture that Paul made sacrifices in the temple after the resurrection of the Messiah?

2. In Leviticus 11, what were the time parameters that God placed on the relevance of the dietary laws He set?

3. What word did God use when describing what violating them would be?

4. In 1 Timothy 4:3, what specifically is the description in that sentence about the meats that those who had "departed from the faith" would forbid?

5. What does sanctified mean?

6. Read Psalm 119. What are 5 words used to describe God's Torah?

7. What is the meaning of the word "fulfilled" in Romans 15:19 and Col 1:25 as Paul uses it in regard to himself? How does this translate when applied to Yeshua in Matt 5:17?

8. IN Matt 5:18-19 what has to happen before even the least commandment of the law passes away?

9. What are the consequences in Matt 5 for those who relax even the least of the Torah commandments and teaches others to?

10. What was the specific behavior being addressed according to verse 5 in Mark 7? Is meat mentioned in Mark 7:1-5?

APPENDIX

◀ Mark 7:19 ▶

Mark 7 Interlinear

	3754 [e]	3756 [e]	1531 [e]		846 [e]	1519 [e]	3588 [e]	2588 [e]		235 [e]	1519 [e]	3588 [e]	2836 [e]	
	hoti	ouk	eisporeuetai		autou	eis	tēn	kardian		all'	eis	tēn	koilian	
19	ὅτι	οὐκ	εἰσπορεύεται		αὐτοῦ	εἰς	τὴν	καρδίαν	,	ἀλλ'	εἰς	τὴν	κοιλίαν	,
	because	not	it enters		of him	into	the	heart		but	into	the	belly	
	Conj	Adv	V-PIM/P-3S		PPro-GM3S	Prep	Art-AFS	N-AFS		Conj	Prep	Art-AFS	N-AFS	

2532 [e]	1519 [e]	3588 [e]	856 [e]	1607 [e]	2511 [e]	3956 [e]	3588 [e]	1033 [e]	
kai	eis	ton	aphedrōna	ekporeuetai	katharizōn	panta	ta	brōmata	
καὶ	εἰς	τὸν	ἀφεδρῶνα	ἐκπορεύεται .	καθαρίζων	πάντα	τὰ	βρώματα	.
and	into	the	draught	goes out	purifying	all	the	food	
Conj	Prep	Art-AMS	N-AMS	V-PIM/P-3S	V-PPA-NMS	Adj-ANP	Art-ANP	N-ANP	

REFERENCES

Peter R. Kraemer, Catholic Church Extension Society (1975), Chicago, Illinois.

ABOUT THE AUTHOR

Robin Gould, D.R.E., LMFT has a Master's Degree in Marriage & Family Therapy and a Doctorate in Religious Education. Practicing as a therapist since 2001, Dr. Gould specializes in Emotionally Focused Couple's Therapy and is currently conferencing on marital health. She is the author of several BEKY books in the BEKY Book series and hosts a radio show on Messianic Lamb Radio. She travels as a lecturer and public speaker enlightening Christians to the Messiah in the Old Testament, as well as emphasizing the relational aspects of the Torah to the Messianic Believer. The proud mother of two wonderful sons, she divides her time between Florida and Vermont with her husband, David. She may be contacted through her website: www.newcovenantpath.com

ACKNOWLEDGEMENTS

Thanks to Dr. Hollisa Alewine for her extensive contributions both in these pages as editor, and off these pages as an optimistic voice leading me to the paths of maturity and wisdom. Thank you for sharing your time and for investing in the community of women, helping their voices be heard for the Glory of the Kingdom. You are sincerely appreciated.

Thank you to Kisha Gallagher for reminding me in all the right ways that the moon is mine. Thank you to Rhonda Sullivan for reminding me that laughter is everything it claims to be. You sisters keep it real and that keeps me going. Thank you, Daniel Vaden, for your loyal, uncompromising friendship in times of war or peace throughout this journey of faith. You are appreciated.

Thanks to my assistant, Staci Bishop, for being smart and on top of things.

To my husband, David, my son, Daniel, my daughter, Tasha, and all of the friends and family I could never properly acknowledge in these pages, thank you for your love and support.

This book celebrates remembrance of Danny Staton for his encouragement of me always, and for his genuine enthusiasm for the Words of the Creator. He is greatly missed. Danny made a difference.